Bibliographic information published by the German National Library:

The German National Library lists this publication in the National Bibliography;
detailed bibliographic data are available on the Internet at http://dnb.dnb.de .

Imprint:

Copyright © 2010 GRIN Verlag, Open Publishing GmbH
Print and binding: Books on Demand GmbH, Norderstedt Germany
ISBN: 9783640597888

This book at GRIN:

http://www.grin.com/en/e-book/149097/the-standardization-of-widget-apis-as-an-
approach-for-overcoming-device

Jakob Sachse

The standardization of Widget-APIs as an approach for overcoming device fragmentation

GRIN Publishing

HTW-Berlin (University of Applied Sciences)

Applied Computer Sience (Master)

2009/2010

The standardization of Widget-APIs
as an approach for overcoming device fragmentation

Jakob Sachse

April 14, 2010

Contents

1 Abstract

Since Apple released the iPhone in 2007 the conversion into a mobile web has accelerated strongly. This paper discusses the challenges resulting from that shift.

The diversity of platforms and device specifications put a heavy burden on developers. While each platform offers an own proprietary API for developing applications it is often desirable to develop applications platform independently. One possible way today is to use web technologies. Although this offers a platform independent API many commonly used system APIs are not accessible. For most applications this is not acceptable since the use of sensors and file I/O is a premise to build modern user experiences.

But now another interesting part of mobile development begins to merge into the sphere of web technology. This is the use of widgets. Widgets were originally designed for desktop use as small single purpose applications but were quickly adapted on the web. Those applications are written using web standards like HTML, CSS and JavaScript.

The widgets we see on the web today can only use the limited JavaScript APIs that is provided by the browsers. Also the W3Cs current widget specification fails to deliver on device APIs, where only packaging and a widgets configuration is specified. That is why new specifications are about to be made and standardized. They describe Widget Engines and their APIs that wrap around modern handsets system APIs.

During the last two years mayor telecommunication companies founded joint ventures like JIL and BONDI to fulfill this goal. Both JIL and BODI have worked out specifications on device APIs and security as well as reference implementations for at least one mobile platform. These results are the input for a new round of widget specification within the W3C.

While there are neither standards nor implementations around today developers have to handle platform diversity themselves. This problem is tackled by some frameworks of which Phonegap and J2ME-Polish are introduced in the conclusion of this paper.

2 Introduction

The shift to a mobile usage of the web has become a mayor influence in advancement of web technology. Pioneering the mobile web was the Apple Newton which in 1996 was the first mobile handset to have a mobile browser [1]. The text-only browser was only capable of displaying a small subset of HTML. Since then the web entered handsets and smartphones till in 2007 Apple boosted the mobile Internet with another pioneering product, the iPhone.

While before the iPhone the Internet was just a feature of a smartphone, the Internet is what the iPhone is build around. The capability to do voice calls became just another feature of a what is now a modern handset. Along with new paradigms in user interface design a new kind of software distribution was introduced.

The first company to react to the iPhone was Google. A hole new mobile operating system that can be seen as Googles response to the iPhone is Android. Android is build on top of the Linux Kernel and follows the same paradigms the iPhone introduced.

- Touch interface

- extensibility via Apps

- App distribution over an online market

As the success of these paradigms became obvious competitors had to react. Today all mayor competitors comply or are at least in convergence to these paradigms.

While the capabilities of todays smartphones become more and more similar the APIs to access those are very different.

PLATFORM	NATIVE APIs	BROWSER ENGINE
iPhone	Objective-C	
Google Android	Custom Java	
RIM Blackberry	Custom Java	HTML + JavaScript + CSS
Windows Phone	.NET Compact Framework	
Palm WebOS	Html5 + Mojo Framework	
SymbianOS	Symbian C++	

Table 1: avaiable APIs across popular platforms

2.1 Widgets

The term widget is ambiguous. Whereas on the one hand the components building a userinterface are called widgets (e.g. buttons, scrollbars etc.) the term also refers to small single purpose applications. This paper refers to widgets in the form of applications. It is these widgets that are run by a widget engine (see 2.2). Their quick accessibility and their focus on a single purpose (i.e. stock ticker, rss reader, weather forecast) makes them well usable in a mobile context where time is short and usability is a key focus.

> "Widgets are a class of client-side web application for displaying and updating local or remote data, packaged in a way to allow a single download and installation on a client machine or device. Widgets typically run as stand-alone applications outside of a web browser, but it is possible to embed them into web pages." [8]

Building widgets on web standards offers a set of advantages of which portability is the most precious. Also there are lots of web developers who already possess the skills needed to develop widgets.

For a widget that is build on top of web technology four considerations are mandatory.

- Device APIs
- Security
- Packaging
- Configuration

2.1.1 Device APIs

Device APIs are needed for accessing the underlaying operating system. This reaches from the phones hardware (e.g. accelerometer, GPS) over the filesystem to phone specific capabilities (e.g. access to contacts or dialing history).

2.1.2 Security

To protect the user against potentially malicious code a security model has to be established in which the user can grand privileges to a certain widgets. A key question in this context is how privileges are granted. It is an open debate on when and how long a privilege is granted.

At a minimum security level the user would grant permissions at widget installation time. At runtime the widget could use its permissions without further notification to the user (this is the security model embraced by Android).

At at much stronger a security model a widget would ask for permission at runtime. While this is more protective to the user it also has the risk of negatively influencing the usability by continuously prompting the user for permissions (this security model is embraced by Symbian S60). A security model has to be a tradeoff between protection and usability.

2.1.3 Packaging

As with web resources in general widgets are composed of multiple documents and resources (i.e. HTML, CSS, images, resources, etc.). It has to be defined what file and folder structure a standardized widget is expected to deliver.

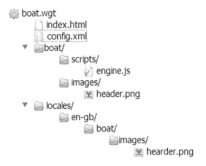

Figure 1: a widgets file and folder structure (W3C)

The W3C Candidate Recommendation Widget Packaging and Configuration defines a folder structure as displayed in figure 1. Also noteworthy is the *.wgt* file-extension which is an archive in zip format. It is used so that widgets are contained within a single file. Other considerations are internationalization and a file that holds the widgets configuration (i.e. config.xml).

2.1.4 Configuration

The configuration of a widget consists of a set of metadata-fields that define how a widget is handled by its runtime. There are fields for display properties (i.e. size, icons) and metadata for the name, version and author of a widget. The runtime uses the metadata for installation and initialization of a widget.

The appendix contains example configurations for widgets that follow different specifications (i.e. W3C Widget 1.0, JIL (Vodafone 360), Nokia WRT).

2.2 Widget Engine

Widget engines provide the runtime environment for widgets. They handle its lifecycle, offer a window for drawing, the user interface and supply APIs that can be used by the widgets code. Most interesting for standardization are widget engines that are build on top of a browser engine. They are capable of rendering HTML/CSS and interpreting JavaScript for doing the business logic.

Another kind of widget engine is one that is build on top of the native OS and uses its UI and event environment. The advantage of those widget engines is that their widgets fit generally better into the userinterface. There are lots of those today but there is little hope that they will ever become standardized. Which in turn binds the widgets to a specific platform.

As pointed out, widget engines provide the application context. For running a widget it is mandatory not only to define the APIs but also to specify the packaging, a security model and a document structure (see 2.1). Of those definitions packaging and security have already been specified by the W3C [4].

7

2.3 Shortcomings of mobile web

As a result of the 1990's browser war, that was won by the Internet Explorer, compliance to web standards was low. But since then standards are gaining influence. Todays modern web browsers are becoming more and more standard compliant. This enables web developers to use the browser a as standardized runtime environment.

Many tasks that ten years ago where fulfilled in standalone applications are today done on the web. The range of applications that are already present on the web reaches out wide. Some of them are classic office applications like word-processing, others are communication utilities like instant messaging, email, calendar or new innovations like Google wave. All those applications are build on top of standardized web technology. Standards and W3C Recommendations (e.g. HTML, CSS, JavaScript) made those innovations possible.

With regard to the mobile web one can notice a different development. While on the classical web, applications move from the native system platform to the web, on mobile handsets applications that make use of the Internet are often not browser driven but native. The following section will elaborate on both technical and marketing reasons for that.

2.3.1 technical reasons

The user interface design for mobile devices has a hole set of own requirements. These requirements are best met by the native OS APIs, since they provide a seamless integration with the operating system. A mobile web browser does not provide the same controls and user experience. Also native Applications have access to system APIs that are yet hidden from the browsers context. Those APIs are of great need to build full featured applications. They provide access to:

- File-System

- Camera

- Contacts

- Acceleration

8

- GEO Location [1]

- Sound Recording

It is those APIs that are heavily used by the most popular Apps. That is why todays Web-Applications can technically not compete with native Apps. But with the introduction of new web standards (HTML5, device APIs, widgets) this is going to change.

2.3.2 marketing reasons

App Stores (e.g. the Apple App Store) serve as a continuous source of revenue where it binds customers and developers close to the platform provider. Software comes in the form of so called Apps. Those Apps are build on top o proprietary APIs that are exclusively controlled by the platform provider. By controlling the only legal way of App distribution a developer is bound to the terms and conditions which force him to share revenue with the platform provider.

PLATFORM	PROVIDER	MARKET	DEVELOPER FEES
iPhone OS	Apple	App Store	99$/year + 30% per sale
Android	Google	Android Market	25$ + 30% per sale
Blackberry	RIM	App World	200$ + 20% per sale
Windows Mobile	Microsoft	Marketplace	99$/year + 30% per sale
WebOS	Palm	App Catalog	30% per sale
SymbianOS	Nokia	OVI Store	50$ + 30% per sale

Table 2: App Markets

As Apple and its rivals gain huge revenues from selling Apps on their stores (see table 2), it is very likely that their interest in rich Internet applications (RIAs) is low. One example for that is how Apple avoids to bring Abobe Flash to the iPhone. While Apple states that this is due to technical issues, it is plausible that Apple will avoid an alternative rich client environment on its platform. [14]

Currently there are lots of games on the Internet that are flash based. Would all those games become accessible on the iPhone a number of customers would probably stick to the free flash games instead of buying games on the App Store. While it is

---

[1] Geolocation API is a W3C Last Call Working Draft and is already implemented in some browsers

easy for Apple to block proprietary runtimes like adobe flash, it will become much harder not to embrace next generation web standards.

Recently there have been efforts to break the bounds that platform providers have build up. It is the network operators as well as hardware manufacturers that have an interest in selling Apps without the close ties to platform providers. Their aim is to provide their clients with applications that come over their own distribution channels (i.e. online stores). A platform independency of these stores would reduce the effort in development and offer a consistent range of apps across different platforms (i.e. develop once deploy everywhere).

3 Current Innovations

This section will highlight the current state in the progress of specifying APIs that allow for interoperable applications. In recent years mayor market players from all over the world have begun to form alliances to tackle the problem of device fragmentation we see today. Their primary aim is to build online markets for applications that are independent of the platform and its provider.

3.1 W3C Recommendation

With the W3C Widget Packaging and Configuration 1.0 Candidate Recommendation there already is a basis to build new specifications upon (see 3.2). The problem today is that while Packaging and Configuration is important other mandatory issues are yet not covered by the W3C. This is the Device APIs that are important to build modern user experiences as well as a security framework that is needed to protect the user against fraugulent misuse of those APIs [1].

3.2 Joint Innovation Labs (JIL)

The Joint Innovation Labs were founded in 2008 by China Mobile Limited, SOFT-BANK, Vodafone. Later in 2009 Verizon Wireless joint JIL.

JIL is specifing API-Specifications in the space of mobile apps and widgets. It offers them royalty-free to operators worldwide. By making their widget specifications avaiable to any wireless company they pursue the goal to reduce the industry fragmentation we see today and to offer a development platform for mobile Web based applications.

The current JIL specifications support the W3C packaging and configuration recommendations (see 3.1). JIL's contribution of the widget API specifications underlines JIL's commitment to support emerging W3C standards.

> "By contributing our widget API specification to the W3C, we are creating the foundation for all wireless service providers and handset manufacturers to participate in a common, open mobile development platform."
> *(JIL CEO, Peters Suh)*

Until today JIL has launched a range of tools including: a common mobile widgets specification, easy-to-use developer kits and SDK's. The industry is reacting positivly to JIL's efforts. After LG Electronics (LG), Research In Motion (RIM), Samsung and Sharp other handset manufacturers (i.e. HTC, Huawei Device, Lenovo and ZTE) announced in February 2010 their plans to provide JIL compliant handsets. [9]

3.3 OMTP BONDI

BONDI is an initiative by the Open Mobile Terminal Platform (OMTP) that was founded in 2008. The OMTP itself was founded in 2004 by AT&T, Deutsche Telekom AG, Orange, Smart Communications, Telecom Italia, Telefonica and Vodafone.[11]

The name BONDI is related to bondi beach (Australia) which is also called a surfers paradise. The initiative defines specifications and APIs for enabling a consistent and secure development of web based applications. To fullfill this goal BONDI is focused on two main issues which are device APIs (see 2.1.1) and a security infrastructure (see 2.1.2).

> "With so many diverse mobile devices and operating systems available in today's marketplace, it can be quite challenging to roll out consistent and compelling new services across such a broad spread. BONDI addresses the need to deliver great services across multiple platforms, whilst ensuring that customers are protected from any risk associated with adopting a more open approach to these systems." *(Reinhard Kreft, Vodafone's Head of Standardisation and Industry Engagements)*

3.4 Wholesale Applications Community

On the mobile world congress 2010 it was announced that twenty-four leading telecommunications operators have formed an alliance for developing the worlds first open platform that delivers applications across all mobile operating systems.

It is the JIL and BONDI members that plan to merge their requirements within the next 12 months under the hood of the so called 'Wholesale Applications Community' (WAC) [12]. In an open letter [13] the Executive Director of the LiMo foundation embraces the formation of the WAC by stating:

"Further to the public announcement of 15 February 2010, I am very pleased to write this open letter to the initiators of the Wholesale Applications Community on behalf of the Board of LiMo Foundation offering a) our full support, b) our committed participation, and c) our immediate practical assistance in a spirit of whole-industry cooperation." *(Morgan Gillis)*

With a joint customer base of 3 billion users the Wholesale Applications Community has the power and influence to finally overcome the fragmentation on the market for mobile apps we see today.

3.5 W3C ongoing work

As JIL and OMTP (BONDI) have both worked out specifications for a web based widget runtime its on the W3C to make a recommendation of those. This work is mainly done within the Device APIs and Policy Working Group (DAP) [6]. Each W3C member can appoint experts as their representatives to the W3C [5]. That means that a W3C working group consists of editors and experts from companies that advocate their own specifications and ideas.

With JIL and OMTP (BONDI) already being large industry alliances it comes down to a handful of specifications that have to be brought together. In addition to JIL and BONDI Nokia has submitted its Nokia Web Runtime (WRT) as input to the working group.

Todays working drafts are in a very early stage. The roadmap for the DAP recommendations is yet not clear. But as the industry pushes forward (e.g. with the foundation of the Wholesale Applications Community) it is likely that the progress within the working group will gain speed.

It can not be in the interest of the W3C that a slow progress in defining new recommendations will lead to de facto standards that alliances in the scale of the Wholesale Applications Community are able to establish.

4 Conclusion

As standardization will certainly take a long time to come a standardized widget runtime is still far off. But with the WAC (see 3.4) merging JIL (see 3.2) and BONDI (see 3.3) specifications within the next 12 months implementations are very likely to be present soon.

4.1 Consequences and Alternatives

As a consequence of a lacking standard, widgets do not run across different platforms. To develop applications platform independent today there are several alternatives of which two are presented here.

4.1.1 J2MEPolish

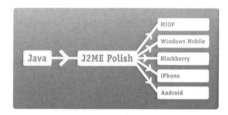

Figure 2: Platform indenpendency through J2ME Polish [15]

J2ME Polish is a Framework that wraps around J2ME. It provides tools and technologies to ease development efforts. One example for this is how design and logic are divided. While the applications logic is implemented in Java the design and animations are done by using CSS. In the context of platform independency the most interesting component of J2ME Polish is its Janus.

> "J2ME Polish supports the global Java ME/J2ME standard and runs on all MIDP enabled handsets. You can also target BlackBerry, Palm, DoJa and WIPI devices with J2ME Polish. Windows Mobile, iPhone and Android platforms are supported natively - you can implement your

application in Java once and J2ME Polish ports it automatically into native applications without having to install a Java Virtual Machine on those platforms. Your application integrates itself like any other native application on your target platform!"

While this sounds easy the reality is not as convenient. There are a couple of porting issues that the developer has to address. For porting a J2ME Application to the iPhone there is a long list of problems that may come up. Also J2ME Polish is not free. Licence fees range from 990Eur to 14,990Eur which makes J2ME Polish less attractive.

4.1.2 PhoneGap

While J2ME Polish is based on Java technology PhoneGap is much more web oriented. Its focus is to embrace web technology for application development. To realize platform independency it provides template projects for each target platform (i.e. Android, iPhone, Windows Mobile, Blackberry). Within these template projects system depended APIs are mapped on JavaScript interfaces that can be used by the PhoneGap application. The interfaces follow the W3C specifications as close as possible. This is also expressed in the project goal:

"An express goal of the PhoneGap project is for the project to not exist."
[16]

Once the different mobile browsers implement the W3C specifications natively there is no need for PhoneGap to further exist. In the meantime the template projects bridge the gap between the different platforms. Instead of using web documents in a widget structure the PhoneGap template projects are to be filled with the web documents (i.e. HTML, CSS, JavaScript) containing the application and then compiled.

After building the projects one gets an installable application for each of the different platforms. With regard to the effort in enabling web technologies to be used for application development this project is most promising.

Also applications build on top of PhoneGap (version 0.8) are allowed to enter the Apple App Store. This has been achieved after direct talks between the PhoneGap developers and Apple.

5 Phonegap API Tests

This section will give an overview of how to use phonegap as a platform independent environment for developing mobile applications. In that context usecases are
presented and sample code that make use of the phonegap APIs is shown. Problems
that may come up when using phonegap are explained.

As phonegap APIs are not natively covered by mobile browsers applications have
to be deployed inside template projects that come with phonegap. Those template projects contain implementations that are injected into the mobile browsers
as JavaScript interfaces.

5.1 Use Case I: Virtual Microscope

The first usecase shows how a virtual microscope can be implemented. It is pre-
sumed that the project has the requirements to be runnable on more than one
mobile platform and to have support for navigation via acceleration data. These
two requirements can be met by using phonegap.

5.1.1 User Interface

First a userinterface is defined by using standard html. There is no restriction upon
how the html document is structured or organized.

```
1  <html>
2  [...]
3    <img id="img" src="img.png"/>
4  [...]
5  </html>
```

Listing 1: Image to be moved

As usual on the web the first page has to be named `index.html`. How the image
itself is retrieved is not covered here since this is not the concern of phonegap.
Instead a placeholder image (`img.png`) is used.

5.1.2 Logic

The image is moved by continuously updating its margin. The margin is a css property that can be accessed by using the HTML DOM API. The following code snippet shows how this is done by providing callback functions that allow for asynchronous updates.

In line 2 defines the success callback that will we called according to the frequency defined in line 11. If an error occurs the error callback (line 8) will be called. The function pointers of the callbacks as well as an option object is passed to the phonegap API in line 12.

```
1  function watchAccel() {
2    function suc(a){
3      a = normalizeAcc(a);
4      document.getElementById('img').style.marginTop = Math.round(a.y)+"px";
5      document.getElementById('img').style.marginLeft = Math.round(a.x)+"px";
6    };
7
8    var fail = function(){};
9    var opt = {};
10
11   opt.frequency = 75;
12   return navigator.accelerometer.watchAcceleration(suc,fail,opt);
13 }
```

Listing 2: Phonegap Accelerometer-API

Within the callback an acceleration object is available that encapsulates the current acceleration for each dimension (a.x, a.y, a.z). The example callback uses another function normalizeAcc(a) to scale the values up into a decent range.

One problem that comes up when using this api is that the range for each dimension is different depending on the device. Android returns values $-2 < x < 2$ whereas on the iPhone $-10 < x < 10$ are returned. This has to be fixed by scaling the values accordingly.

17

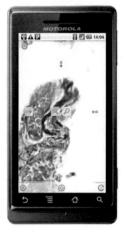

Figure 3: PhoneGap App on Android and iPhone

As shown in figure 3 the application runs on the iPhone as well as on Android. It uses acceleration data generated by both phones sensors and made avaiable inside the web context by phonegap.

5.2 Use Case II: Shop Finder

For implementing a location based service a geo API is necessary. While the W3C has specified an API for that purpose [2] its not yet implemented on all mobile browsers. That is why phonegap provides an api that follows the W3C specification.

Certainly it is upon the backend to provide interesting services. But while the backend is not the focus of this paper the following example shows how a link to a third party service (in this case google maps) can be generated.

The link will enclose longitude and latitude information that will correspond to the current position. Additionally a search query can be specified that will trigger a local search on that position.

5.2.1 Reading geolocation

To start with an anchor is specified. The `href` attribute is set to '#' which makes the link void when the page loads.

```
1  <html>
2  [...]
3  <a id="googleMapsLink" href="#">display shops in this area</a>
4  [...]
5  </html>
```

Listing 3: PhoneGap Geolocation-Link

To generate the url to google maps the phonegap API is called. The asynchronous call `navigator.geolocation.getCurrentPosition` takes two arguments which are references to callback functions. When the underlaying system has determined the current postion the success callback is invoked. In case of a possible failure the error function will be called.

Within the success callback an object that reflects the current position is provided. As to be seen in line 5 the object contains the properties latitude and longitude that are used to generate the url. To make google search for shops in the specified area a query parameter is set. After the link is generated it is set to the `href` attribute using jQuery (line 7).

```
1  var getLocation = function() {
2    var suc = function(p){
3      var q="shop";
4      var mapsLinkPre="http://maps.google.com/maps?f=q&source=s_q&hl=de&q="+q;
5      var params="&geocode=&sll="+p.coords.latitude+","+p.coords.longitude;
6      var mapsLinkPost="&sspn=0.043975,0.077162&ie=UTF8&t=h&z=14";
7      $("#googleMapsLink").attr("href",mapsLinkPre+params+mapsLinkPost);
8    }
9
10   var fail = function(){}
11
12   navigator.geolocation.getCurrentPosition(suc,fail);
13 }
```

Listing 4: PhoneGap Geolocation-API

5.3 Phonegap Deployment

Even though the phonegap APIs are (with some exceptions) equal the deployment of a phonegap application is very dependent on its target platform. Phonegap comes with a template project for each supported platform. There are two ways of getting those. First there are stable releases on the phonegap website. One can download them and unpack the template projects.

Alternatively one can use GIT. GIT is an open source version control system. The template projects are hosted within a git repository. To gain a working copy of the repository one needs to install GIT and clone the repository.

```
1  //for the iPhone template
2  git clone git://github.com/phonegap/phonegap-iphone.git
3
4  //for the Android template
5  git clone git://github.com/phonegap/phonegap-android.git
```

Listing 5: Getting a phonegap working copy

After the submodules are initialized and updated the template projects are ready to be build. For the iPhone template this is done by using `make`. The build results in a `PhoneGapLibInstaller.pkg` file being generated. Starting this file will pull up XCode that then has a phonegap template project installed. The project must be filled with the application documents which are put inside a `www` named directory inside the project. To make the application look unique it is recommended to add a custom icon. This is done like on any other iPhone project. After these final customizations are done one can build and install the application on the iPhone/Simulator.

Building the Android project is done differently. The working copy of the Android submodule comes with a ruby script that will call `ant` to build the template project (on a windows system). The script takes arguments that point to the framework directory, `www` folder and application name. The result is a project that can be imported into eclipse. As with the iPhone project one can add a custom icon and name for the application.

It can be seen that although the web APIs are equal there is still some overhead to create the target applications. But while there are no common native widget APIs available this effort is inevitably.

20

Web References

1. FIRST TRUE WEB BROWSER FOR NEWTON. *Pen Computing Magazine.*
   http://www.pencomputing.com/archive/PCM_11/nethopper.html

2. GEOLOCATION API SPECIFICATION. *W3C.*
   http://www.w3.org/TR/geolocation-API/

3. HTML 5. *W3C.*
   http://www.w3.org/TR/html5/

4. WIDGET PACKAGING AND CONFIGURATION. *W3C.*
   http://www.w3.org/TR/widgets/

5. W3C MEMBERSHIP. *W3C.*
   http://www.w3.org/Consortium/membership

6. DEVICE APIS AND POLICY WORKING GROUP. *W3C.*
   http://www.w3.org/2009/dap/

7. JOINT INNOVATION LAB (JIL).
   http://www.jil.org/

8. WIDGET SYSTEM HIGH LEVEL TECHNICAL SPECIFICATION. JOINT INNOVATION LAB (JIL).
   http://dev.mmarket.com/JIL+Widget+System+High+Level+Technical+Specification+-+Widget+Formats

9. JOINT INNOVATION LAB GIBT WIDGET-API-SPEZIFIKATIONEN FREI UND BRINGT SIE IN W3C EIN. PRESSEPORTAL.DE
   http://www.presseportal.de/pm/77530/1562154/jil_joint_innovation_lab

10. BONDI. OPEN MOBILE TERMINAL PLATFORM (OMTP).
    http://bondi.omtp.org

11. FÜHRENDE MOBILNETZBETREIBER ARBEITEN GEMEINSAM AN DER UMSETZUNG REICHHALTIGER, MOBILER INTERNETDIENSTE. PRESSEPORTAL.DE
    http://www.presseportal.de/pm/66900/1220964/omtp_ltd

12. WHOLESALE APPLICATIONS COMMUNITY.
    http://www.wholesaleappcommunity.com/

13. OPEN LETTER TO THE WHOLESALE APPLICATIONS COMMUNITY.

WWW.LIMOFOUNDATION.ORG
http://www.limofoundation.org/en/Press-Releases/open-letter-to-the-wholesale-applications-co

14. ADOBE ENGAGES APPLE IN PASSIVE AGGRESSIVE WARFARE WITH IPHONE'S
    FLASH MESSAGE. *engadget.com.*
    http://www.engadget.com/2009/11/02/adobe-engages-apple-in-passive-aggressive-warfare-with-iph

15. J2ME POLISH: DOCUMENTATION. *J2ME Polish.*
    http://www.j2mepolish.org/cms/leftsection/documentation/platforms.html

16. *PhoneGap*
    http://phonegap.com/

Appendix

```xml
1 <?xml version="1.0" encoding="UTF-8"?>
2
3 <widget xmlns      = "http://www.w3.org/ns/widgets"
4         id         = "http://example.org/exampleWidget"
5         version    = "2.0 Beta"
6         height     = "320"
7         width      = "240"
8         viewmodes  = "widget">
9
10   <name short="Example 2.0">My Awesome Application</name>
11
12   <description>
13         It asks you your name, and says hi!
14   </description>
15
16   <feature name="http://example.com/camera">
17     <param name="autofocus" value="true"/>
18   </feature>
19
20   <preference name    = "apikey"
21               value   = "ea31ad3a23fd2f"
22               readonly = "true" />
23
24   <author href="http://foo-bar.example.org/" email="foo-bar@example.org">
25         Foo Bar Corp
26   </author>
27
28   <icon src="icons/icon_64.png"/>
29
30   <content src="myWidget.html"/>
31
32   <license>MIT License</license>
33 </widget>
```

Listing 6: W3C config.xml

```xml
1  <?xml version="1.0" encoding="UTF-8"?>
2
3  <widget dockable="yes">
4    <widgetname>Widget Example</widgetname>
5    <description>It asks you your name, and says hi!</description>
6    <icon src="icon_64.png" />
7
8    <width>240</width>
9    <height>320</height>
10
11   <author>
12     <name>Foo Bar Corp</name>
13   </author>
14
15   <id>
16     <name>My Awesome Application</name>
17     <revised>2009-04-08</revised>
18   </id>
19 </widget>
```

Listing 7: Vodafone 360 config.xml

```
1  <?xml version="1.0" encoding="utf-8" ?>
2  <widget xmlns="http://www.jil.org/ns/widgets"
3    id="http://jil.org/myWidget"
4    version="01.00.Beta"
5    height="150"
6    width="100">
7
8      <name>Widget Example</name>
9      <description>It asks you your name, and says hi!</description>
10     <author email="foobar@corp.com">Foo Bar Corp</author>
11     <icon src="icon_64.png"/>
12
13     <license href="http://creativecommons.org/licenses/by/3.0/">
14     Creative Commons Attribution License
15     </license>
16
17     <access network="true" localfs="true" remote_scripts="false"/>
18     <content src="myWidgetContent.html"/>
19     <update href="http://www.jil.org/widgets/" period="1"/>
20     <feature name="http://jil.org/apis/api.DeviceInfo" required="true"/>
21     <feature name="http://jil.org/apis/api.CalendarItem" required="false"/>
22     <maximum_display_mode height="300" width="200"/>
23     <billing required="true"/>
24
25  </widget>
```

Listing 8: JIL config.xml

```
1  <?xml version="1.0" encoding="UTF-8"?>
2  <!DOCTYPE plist PUBLIC "-//Nokia//DTD PLIST 1.0//EN"
3  "http://www.nokia.com/DTDs/plist-1.0.dtd">
4    <plist version="1.0">
5      <dict>
6        <key>DisplayName</key>
7        <string>HelloWRT</string>
8
9        <key>Identifier</key>
10       <string>com.HelloWRT.basic.widget</string>
11
12       <key>Version</key>
13       <string>1.0</string>
14
15       <key>MainHTML</key>
16       <string>index.html</string>
17
18       <key>MiniViewEnabled</key>
19       <false/>
20     </dict>
21   </plist>
```

Listing 9: Nokia Web Runtime info.plist

YOUR KNOWLEDGE HAS VALUE

- We will publish your bachelor's and master's thesis, essays and papers

- Your own eBook and book - sold worldwide in all relevant shops

- Earn money with each sale

Upload your text at www.GRIN.com and publish for free